LIFE CYCLE OF A

LADYBUG

By Kirsty Holmes

KidHaven PUBLISHING

LIFE CYCLES

Words that look like **this** can be found in the glossary on page 24.

Published in 2022 by
KidHaven Publishing, an Imprint of Greenhaven Publishing, LLC
353 3rd Avenue
Suite 255
New York, NY 10010

Edited by: Robin Twiddy
Designed by: Brandon Mattless

Cataloging-in-Publication Data

Names: Holmes, Kirsty.
Title: Life cycle of a ladybug / Kirsty Holmes.
Description: New York : KidHaven Publishing, 2022. | Series: Life cycles | Includes glossary and index.
Identifiers: ISBN 9781534537941 (pbk.) | ISBN 9781534537965 (library bound) | ISBN 9781534537958 (6 pack) | ISBN 9781534537972 (ebook)
Subjects: LCSH: Ladybugs--Juvenile literature. | Ladybugs--Life cycles--Juvenile literature.
Classification: LCC QL596.C65 H68 2022 | DDC 595.76'9--dc23

Printed in the United States of America

CPSIA compliance information: Batch #CSKH22: For further information contact Greenhaven Publishing LLC, New York, New York at 1-844-317-7404.

PHOTO CREDITS

All images are courtesy of shutterstock.com, unless otherwise specified. With thanks to Getty Images, Thinkstock Photo and iStockphoto. Front Cover & 1 – pernsanitzfoto, irin-k. 2 – Leonid Ikan. 3 – KKphotographer, Mks.G.A, Christiane Godin. 4 – GSK919, StockImageFactory.com. 5 – India Picture, michaeljung, StockImageFactory.com. 6 – Antonio Gravante. 7 – AdaCo. 8 – Brett Hondow. 9 – KKphotographer, schankz. 10 – Henri Koskinen. 11 – thatmacroguy. 12 – ozgur kerem bulur. 13 – matunka. 14 – JonRichfield. 15 – Protasov AN. 16 – Mks.G.A, JFCerez. 17 – Rachasie. 18 – LedyX, lewalp, aaltair. 19 – vitek3ds, max dallocco, TungCheung, DenisNata. 20 – Wattlebird. 21 – Christiane Godin. 22 – mchin, Anest, Gilles San Martin. 23 – Young Swee Ming, Henri Koskinen, Ger Bosma Photos.

CONTENTS

Page 4 What Is a Life Cycle?
Page 6 Lovely Ladybugs
Page 8 Excellent Eggs
Page 10 Loads of Larvae
Page 12 Perfect Pupae
Page 14 Lovely Ladybugs
Page 16 Life as a Ladybug
Page 18 Fun Facts About Ladybugs
Page 20 The End of Life as a Ladybug
Page 22 The Life Cycle
Page 24 Glossary and Index

WHAT IS A LIFE CYCLE?

All living things have a life cycle. They are all born, they all grow bigger, and their bodies change.

Teenager

Adult

When they are fully grown, they have **offspring** of their own. In the end, all living things die. This is the life cycle.

Elderly Person

LOVELY LADYBUGS

A ladybug is a type of beetle. This means it is an insect, with six legs and hard front wings. These wings are not used for flying. They cover and protect a soft pair of wings underneath.

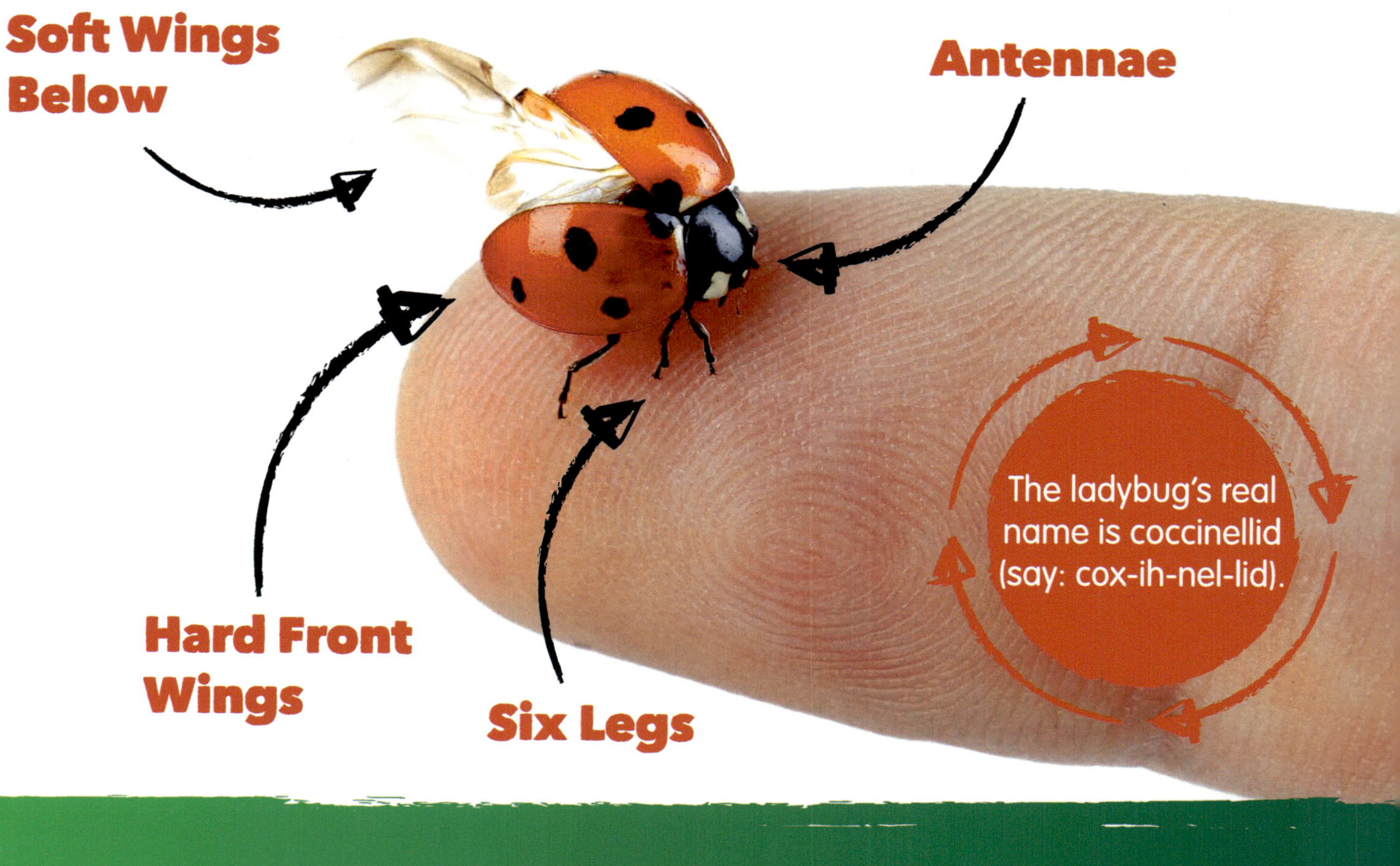

The ladybug's real name is coccinellid (say: cox-ih-nel-lid).

Ladybugs are often red with black spots, but they can also come in other bright patterns. These bright colors scare off **predators**. Ladybugs are very small. The largest they can grow is around 0.4 inch (1 cm) long.

EXCELLENT EGGS

Female Ladybug Laying Eggs

In the summer months, a female ladybug can lay around 1,000 eggs. The female lays her eggs in groups, usually on the underside of a leaf. The eggs are orange or yellow.

The female ladybug will often lay her eggs close to a **colony** of aphids. Aphids are small insects with soft bodies. They drink the **sap** of plants. They are also a ladybug's favorite food!

LOADS OF LARVAE

After four to ten days, the eggs hatch. The **larvae** come out of the eggs, but they don't look like ladybugs yet. Larvae may be black, brown, or gray, and they may have yellow and orange patches.

This larva has **shed** its skin. Can you see the larva and the old skin?

The larvae are very hungry and will eat lots of aphids. As the larvae grow, they get too big for their skins. They grow a new skin underneath, then shed the old skin.

PERFECT PUPAE

When the larvae have shed their skins for the last time, they find a leaf to attach themselves to. They don't move or eat. They change from larvae to **pupae.**

Pupae stay still for up to two weeks. Inside, the bodies of the larvae are changing. They are making their wings and legs, ready to become adults.

LOVELY LADYBUGS

The adult ladybug is pale and soft when it comes out. As it dries, its outer wings harden. The ladybug gets its color now, too.

This newly hatched adult is drying in the sun.

Ladybugs come in different colors, and each **species** has its own pattern. Most ladybugs are red, black, orange, or yellow. Many ladybug species have spots, but some have stripes instead.

LIFE AS A LADYBUG

Adult ladybugs look for food. They are **omnivores** and they like to eat aphids, whiteflies, and mealybugs. Some species like to eat caterpillars. They also eat plants, pollen, nectar, and **fungi**.

Aphids eat plants and **crops**. Gardeners and farmers like ladybugs to live in their gardens because ladybugs eat aphids. Ladybugs can eat up to 50 aphids each day. This keeps the plants and crops safe.

FUN FACTS ABOUT LADYBUGS

• Ladybugs are also known as ladybirds and lady beetles.

• There are over 6,000 different types of ladybugs in the world.

• The ladybird spider has a red **abdomen** and looks a bit like a ladybug.

• Ladybugs smell through their antennae and their feet!

Ladybugs live on every continent except Antarctica.

THE END OF LIFE AS A LADYBUG

These ladybugs are **hibernating** underneath this light.

Most ladybugs live for around one year. In the winter, they gather together in a group. This helps them keep warm. Most will die, but the ones that live will **mate** again in the spring.

Many predators like to eat ladybugs. Toads catch them on their long, sticky tongues. Spiders trap them in their webs, and birds catch them in the air.

This spider has caught a tasty lunch.

THE LIFE CYCLE

The egg hatches into a larva. This becomes a pupa and changes into an adult ladybug.

The adult goes on to have offspring of its own.

GLOSSARY

abdomen	the rear section of an insect's body
colony	a group of animals living in one place
crop	a plant that is grown on a large scale to be eaten or used
fungi	living things that look like plants but have no flowers
hibernate	to spend the winter sleeping or in a dormant state to save energy
larvae	young animals that must grow and change form before they become adults
mate	to produce young with an animal of the same species
offspring	the young of an animal or plant
omnivore	an animal that eats both plants and other animals
predator	an animal that hunts other animals for food
pupae	insects at the stage of change between larvae and adult
sap	a sweet liquid found in plants
shed	to remove and replace the skin or shell with another one that has grown underneath
species	a group of very similar animals or plants that can create young together

INDEX

aphids 9, 11, 16-17
eggs 8-10, 22
feet 19
ladybird spiders 18
larvae 10-13, 22
predators 7, 21
pupae 12-13, 22-23
spots 7, 15
wings 6, 13-14